ON THE

Syriac Orthodox Church

JOACHIM SANISH

INDIA • SINGAPORE • MALAYSIA

ISBN
Paperback : 979-8-89233-792-2
Hardcase: 979-8-89277-312-6

Glory to God in the highest, And on earth peace, goodwill toward men!"

St. Luke 2: 14

Thank our Lord and our God, Jesus Christ, for enabling his servant to write about his glory.

In loving memory of my grandfather, Mr. P.K. George.

Contents

Preface

In the beginning of all this, I had a thought that an encyclopaedia was needed for the Holy Church, our mother, for there was not much information that one could find due to the scarcity of books concerning the matters and of online resources. Therefore, I set to making this book for you, my dear brethren in Christ, so that one should know about the Syriac Orthodox Church. Therefore, I hope that you enjoy reading and that you get all the information you were seeking.

Signed,

Joachim Sanish

June 2022

CATHOLICATE OF JACOBITE SYRIAN CHRISTIAN CHURCH
UNDER THE HOLY SEE OF ANTIOCH & ALL THE EAST
PATRIARCHAL CENTRE, PUTHENCRUZ P. O.
ERNAKULAM, KERALA, INDIA 682 308
Email : patriarchalcentre@yahoo.com

BY THE GRACE OF GOD
BASELIUS THOMAS I
CATHOLICOSE AND ANGAMALY
DIOCESAN METROPOLITAN

No : SM-25/2023

Date

Blessings to our beloved Joachim Sanish

"On the Syriac Orthodox Church", by Joachim Sanish, is the book that which provides the beginners an ample knowledge about the Church and her doctrines. We are so happy that the author Joachim Sanish is the grandson of our beloved Rev. Fr. Geevarghese Vazhattil from our Angamaly Diocese. We wish our young writer God's blessings and good wishes for this work. May God bless you to write more literatures for the glory of our God and our Holy Church.

23.10.2023
Patriarchal Centre
Puthencruz

Baselios Thomas I Catholicose

JACOBITE SYRIAN CHRISTIAN CHURCH

(Under the Holy Apostolic See of Antioch & all the East)

JOSEPH MOR GREGORIOS
MALANKARA METHRAPOLITHA
(METROPOLITAN TRUSTEE)

16 December, 2023

Blessings to our beloved spiritual son Master Joachim Sanish and Family

I am delighted to extend my heartfelt congratulations to Master Joachim Sanish on the completion of your remarkable book, "On the Syrian Orthodox Church." Your dedication to explore the doctrine of the Virgin Mary is truly touching and commendable. It is inspiring to witness someone of your age delve into such profound subjects with passion and insight.

Your efforts in contributing to the understanding of our Church and its faith are invaluable, and I commend you for the depth of your work. May your journey as a young author continue to be filled with wisdom, growth, and the joy of sharing your love for the Syrian Orthodox Church.

May your journey continue to be a beacon of inspiration for others and may your contributions to the Syriac Orthodox Church leave a lasting impact.

Wishing you continued success in your endeavors and looking forward to witnessing the positive impact your contributions will undoubtedly have on others.

Warm regards and blessings to you as well.

Joseph Gregorios Metropolitan
Malankara Methrapolitha

Patriarchal Centre, Puthencruz, Ernakulam, Kerala - 682 308, South India Ph : 2732804, 9846004461 E-mail : hasiojosephg@gmail.com
Bishop's House, Kyomtha Seminary, Thiruvamkulam, Kerala 682 305 Ph : 9847466000, Email : kyomthaseminary@gmail.com,

JACOBITE SYRIAN CHRISTIAN CHURCH

(UNDER THE HOLY APOSTOLIC SEE OF ANTIOCH AND ALL THE EAST)

(ANGAMALY DIOCESE)

Dr. ANTHIMOS MATTHEWS
Angamaly Diocese - Muvattupuzha Region

E-mail : anthimosmatthews@gmail.com

Blessing to our dearly beloved Joachim Sanish

At the very outset, I would like to congratulate Joachim Sanish for his book entitled "On the Syriac Orthodox Church". This work proves the author's commitment and dedication to our Holy Syriac Orthodox Church and her rich traditions. The book discusses in short chapters about the Faith, Doctrines, Theology and History of our Syriac Orthodox Church. The volume of contents is very precise, therefore, this would help our budding generation to learn about the Holy Syriac Orthodox Church. The reader friendly writing skills and clarity in the presentations are few highlights of this Book.

I am so glad to know that Joachim Sanish is the grandson of our dearly beloved Rev. Fr. Geevarghese Vazhattil, who serves in our Angamaly Diocese, having so much passion for the spiritual life. I wish God's abundant blessing upon this young devotee in order to bring up with many more books for the glory of our Syriac Orthodox Church.

23.10.2023
Patriarchal Centre
Puthencruz

Anthimos Matthews Metropolitan

H.G Mathews Mor Timotheos
Metropolitan, Mor Gabriel Monastery
Veettoor, Muvattupuzha,
Ernakulam, Kerala

Date : 01-12-2023

I am deeply moved and filled with joy as I hold in my hands the profound work of young Joachim Sanish, "On the Syriac Orthodox Church.", which was introduced to me by his grandfather Rev. Fr. Geevarghese Vazhattiil. I am so happy to learn that he started to write books at the age of Eight (8) and now at age of 10 he has completed this book which is commendable. The preface alone reveals a passionate and earnest desire to serve the Holy Mother Church, recognizing the scarcity of resources dedicated to our cherished faith.

Joachim's effort to distill complex doctrines into a form accessible to all is truly remarkable. His interpretation of the Doctrine of the Trinity, the Doctrine of the First Sin, and many others, showcases not only his understanding but also his dedication to sharing this knowledge with others. It is evident that he is driven by a pure love for the Church.

As a bishop, I am delighted to extend my blessings and heartfelt wishes to young Joachim Sanish. May the wisdom that flows from these pages continue to enlighten hearts and minds, guiding them in the path of faith. May he continue to grow in the knowledge and love of our Lord, and may his future be filled with divine grace and countless opportunities to serve the Universal Syrian Orthodox Church.

May Joachim's journey be a source of inspiration for others, and may his contributions to the Church serve as a testament to the power of youthful dedication and love for the faith.

With warmest regards and heartfelt blessings,

Timotheos Mathews

Metropolitan

Chapter One

Doctrine of The Most Holy Trinity

Syriac Icon of Theophany[1]

1 Reference from DSS (Department of Syriac Studies)

The Syriac Orthodox Church has a very strong doctrine about the existence of the Trinity. We believe that God is 3 divine persons in one divine essence. The 3 persons are: God the Father, God the Son, and God the Holy Spirit. The Son is eternally begotten of the Father before the existence of time and space, being His Son. The Holy Spirit eternally proceeds from the Father and also takes from the Son. Even though the Trinity is 3 in person, it is one in essence; therefore, there is only one God. It is best not to use analogies to describe the Trinity. Most analogies lead to potential heresy. A light analogy may be used, such as that of the sun, its rays, and its heat. The sun symbolises the Father. The rays symbolise the son, who is born of the Father, just as the rays are born of the sun. The heat symbolises the Holy Spirit, as heat proceeds from the sun and also, one cannot see heat but can only feel it. However, it is best not to delve deeper into these simple analogies, as heresy may be discovered. For example, in our simple analogy of the sun, we discover that the analogy is Arian in nature, for the sun's rays and heat are its creations. Again, let us take the simple analogy of the three-leaf clover, 3 leaves, one plant. However, upon further discovery, that is Partialism, for each leaf is one-third of the plant, and not the whole plant itself. There are many analogies that could be used, but we'd rather not mention them, for not only would it take a long time, but also the reader might become confused.

Chapter Two

Doctrine of Ancestral (Original) Sin

The first sin of Adam and Eve, according to the biblical narrative in Genesis 3, involved disobedience to God's command. God had instructed them not to eat the fruit from the tree of the knowledge of good and evil in the Garden of Eden (Genesis 2:17). However, influenced by the serpent, Eve ate the forbidden fruit and also persuaded Adam to do the same. This act of disobedience, often referred to as the fall of man, led to their expulsion from the Garden of Eden and introduced sin and death into the world. Now, what is ancestral sin? Now when Adam and Eve first sinned against God, they were enslaved by sin. And, as the apostle St. Paul writes in Romans 6:23, the wages of sin is death. Therefore, because of that first sin which allowed sin itself to enter the world, not only Adam and Eve, but also the entire human race was enslaved by sin and death. Sin and death became a part of the human nature itself. When a human child is born into the world, (s)he is already caught up in sin and is liable to death.

Orthodox Icon of the Expulsion from Paradise

Chapter Three

Doctrine of The Nature of Christ

A fundamental element of Syriac Orthodox Christology is the doctrine of monophysitism (also called miaphysitism). It teaches that God the Son, our Lord Jesus Christ, has one incarnate nature, in which He is fully God and fully man. Now, before His incarnation, we know that He is fully God. Now, after His incarnation, He has united his humanity with His divinity. This union of divinity with humanity causes His one incarnate nature. Rather than the creation of a separate nature within the same Person, we believe in the union of His humanity and divinity, which is one of the reasons for the Incarnation. The Church also accepts the term, 'union of 2 natures.' It is very risky to discuss the nature of Christ. The Christological doctrine of monophysitism is the main point of disagreement between the Oriental Orthodox churches and the more mainstream churches such as the Catholic and Eastern Orthodox churches. The Oriental Orthodox accept monophysitism, while the mainstream churches reject it. There was a wave of persecution against the Oriental Orthodox during the fifth and sixth centuries AD. The Syriac Orthodox Church is Oriental Orthodox in her Christology.

Syriac Icon of Christ

It is important to understand the difference between the doctrine of monophysitism and the heresy of

Eutychianism. Eutychianism, named after its founder, the heretic Eutyches, espouses that Christ had one nature, but that his humanity was consumed by his divinity. The Syriac Orthodox Church rejects and condemns this teaching as heresy. However, many mainstream Christians have mistaken the Oriental Orthodox as confessors of Eutychianism. Also, because of this mistake, Eutychianism has been renamed monophysitism. Hence comes the name miaphysitism.

Chapter Four

Doctrine of The Incarnation

We believe that God the Son, our Lord Jesus Christ, took the fashion of mortal flesh and came to the earth. He was born of and received His humanity from His mother, the Holy Virgin Mary. He, now being a man, taught mankind the path of righteousness. But humanity, ridiculed of the divine things He spoke of, crucified Him on the cross, thus killing His humanity. Through His death, our Lord atoned for the sin of all of humanity.

His sacrifice was timeless and was for all people, both Jew and Gentile. According to the teachings of St. Severus, patriarch of Antioch (465-538 AD), even though His spirit departed from His flesh, His divinity did not. Rather, His divinity remained united with both His flesh and His spirit. He descended into Sheol, the abode of the dead, and having preached His Gospel there, he set free Adam and all the dead. Three days after His death, He arose from the dead, glorious with the authority of His divinity. He liberated the human race from its sinful nature. After these things, He ascended into heaven and sent the Holy Spirit upon His apostles that they may preach His Gospel throughout the world. He also promised us that He would return one day, to judge the living and the dead. Now, why did the Lord suffer all these things? When man strayed away to Satan, God wanted to retrieve man. But he had to pay a price, the price was a man's life. How did God pay this price? By becoming a man and sacrificing his life for us. Our atonement was won by the sacrifice of Christ. Syriac Icon of the Descent into Hades (Resurrection)

Chapter Five

Doctrine of The Mother of God

The virginal birth of Christ is foretold in the prophecy of Isaiah (7:14), which states, "Therefore the Lord Himself will give you a sign: Behold, the virgin shall conceive and bear a Son, and shall call His name Immanuel." This virgin is Mary. There are many prototypes of the Holy Virgin Mary in the Old Testament. The most commonly recognised is the burning bush which Moses saw (Exodus 3:2). The bush was on fire, yet it was not burnt nor was it consumed. Another is the staff of Aaron (Numbers 17:8). The staff of Aaron, although it was made of dry wood, blossomed. So on, so forth go the prototypes of the Holy Virgin Mary.

The right of the Holy Virgin Mary to be called and venerated as the Mother of God has been tested and debated throughout time. The first major opposition was the heresy of Nestorianism. There was great dispute, and therefore, 159 bishops gathered at the Council of Ephesus, in 431 AD, to discuss this matter. Eventually, due to the work of fathers such as St. Cyril, pope of Alexandria, and Celestine I, pope of Rome, Nestorianism was condemned as heresy, and the title of the Holy Virgin Mary as the Mother of God was further cemented. Even now there are traces of opposition, especially among Protestants, not only against this particular title of the Holy Virgin Mary but also against her veneration wholly. Therefore, let us point to Elisabeth's words (St. Luke 1:43), "But why is this granted to me, that the mother of my Lord should come to me?" Throughout the Old Testament, God is referred to as the Lord. This was due to fear of pronouncing the divine name. Therefore, when Elisabeth calls Mary the mother of her Lord (point to the capitalisation of the letter L), she is calling her the mother of her God. Also, note that it is not really her who is speaking, but the Holy Spirit through her.

The perpetual virginity of the Holy Virgin Mary is an official doctrine of the Church. It is pointed to in the prophecy of Ezekiel (44:1-3), "Then He brought me back to the outer gate of the sanctuary which faces toward the east, but it was shut. And the Lord said to me, 'This gate shall be shut; it shall not be opened, and no man shall enter by it, because the Lord God of Israel has entered by it; therefore it shall be shut.'" The gate points to the Holy Virgin Mary, through whose womb the Lord God of Israel has entered; therefore, it shall be shut forever.

The Scriptures first tell of Mary in the Gospel according to St. Matthew the Apostle. The first verse recording her name is St. Matthew 1:18. Though the Bible has no record of the parents of the Virgin, the Syriac Orthodox Church believes that she was born to St. Joachim and St. Anna.

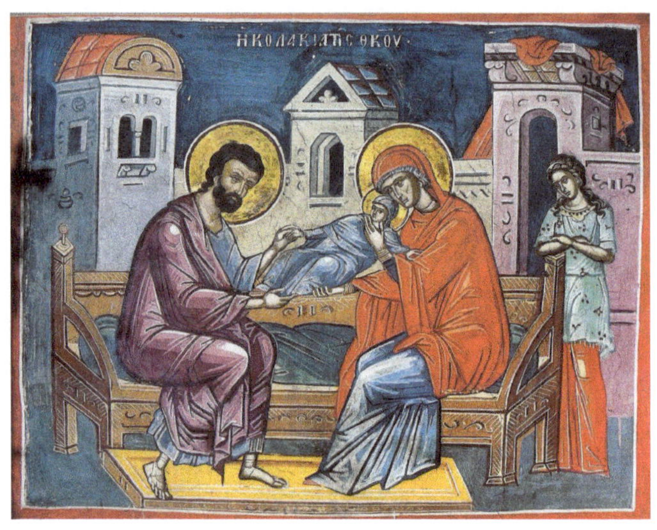

Orthodox Icon of St. Joachim and St. Anna with the Infant Virgin

This is the belief of the Syriac Orthodox Church about the Nativity of Mary.

St. Joachim and his wife, St. Anna, though they were married for several years, were without a child. Both being righteous and obedient to the Lord entreated God for a child, but their plea was not answered. The residents of the town of Nazareth, where they dwelt, believed that couples who were childless for many years were cursed by the Lord. Once, when St. Joachim was entering the temple of Jerusalem, some men who were bringing their offerings saw him and mocked him for being unfruitful. The elderly man, full of sorrow when he heard the reprimand, left the temple and departed into the wilderness to fast and pray for an offspring. When his wife, St. Anna, heard that her husband had left for the desert, she too was heartbroken and began praying for a child. After days and days, the Lord saw their grief and answered their prayers. Then, an angel was sent to St. Anna. As she was on her knees praying, the angel appeared to her and told her that she would bear a daughter and that her child's name would be known throughout the globe. Overjoyed, St. Anna arose and glorified the Lord. Another angel later appeared to St. Joachim as well and told him the same message. St. Anna sent word to her husband about the news, and he returned home, joyously. The couple met at the Golden Gate, as instructed by the angels, and embraced. During their embrace, St. Anna conceived in her womb, the infant Mary.

Orthodox Icon of the Conception of the Theotokos.

Later, she gave birth to a daughter, as the angels had said, and they named her Mary. And thus, the Mother of God was born.

Orthodox Icon of the Nativity of the Theotokos

Now, this is how she conceived Christ. St. Luke the Evangelist writes in his Gospel about the Annunciation to the Theotokos (St. Luke 1:26-38). The archangel St. Gabriel is sent. During the annunciation of the glorious message of the future-Incarnation, the Holy Spirit came upon Mary, and she was cleansed of all her ancestral impurity and conceived in her womb the Infant Christ.

Syriac Icon of the Annunciation to the Theotokos

Later, as St. Matthew writes in his Gospel, St. Joseph, who was betrothed to the virgin, was a just and righteous man, and when he found out that his betrothed was pregnant, he thought that she had lain with another man and wanted to divorce her. The Church has a hymn that holds a record of the dispute between St. Joseph and the Mother of God, as he brings the bill of divorce. According to St. Matthew 1:20-21, that night after their dispute, as St. Joseph lay asleep in bed, an angel appeared to him and said: "Joseph, son of David, do not be afraid to take to you Mary your wife, for that which is conceived in her is that of the Holy Spirit. And she will bring forth a Son, and you shall call His name JESUS, for He will save his people from their sins."

Syriac Icon of the Revelation of St. Joseph the Betrothed[2]

When St. Joseph arose the next day, he was overjoyed and accepted the Theotokos as his wife. Later, as said in St. Luke 1:36, Elizabeth, Mary's cousin, was found with Infant John. The cheerful Mary visited the house of Zacharias and Elizabeth. As the Theotokos approached their doorstep and greeted her cousin, the child in Elizabeth's womb leapt with merriment. Elizabeth, being filled with the Holy Spirit, cried out to the Holy Virgin,

2 Reference from DSS (Department of Syriac Studies)

saying: "Blessed are you among women, and blessed is the fruit of your womb! But why is this granted to me, that the mother of my Lord should come to me? For indeed, as soon as the voice of your greeting sounded in my ears, the babe leapt in my womb for joy. Blessed is she who believed, for there will be a fulfilment of those things which were told to her from the Lord." (St. Luke 1:39-45)

Orthodox Icon of the Visitation of the Virgin[3]

3 Reference from DSS Icons

St. Luke then mentions the Theotokos when he writes about the Nativity of Christ (St. Luke 2:1-20). Later, St. John the Apostle and Theologian writes in his Gospel about the Wedding of Cana, where he too mentions the Mother of God (St. John 2:1-12). Then we come to St. John 19, to the incident of the Crucifixion, where Christ tells his mother, Mary, as he hangs on the cross: "Woman, behold your son" (St. John 19:26) and to the beloved disciple, St. John: "Behold your mother," thus entrusting the Holy Virgin into the care of St. John. Mary suffered intolerable agony as the earthly ministry of her son drew near.

Syriac Icon of the Crucifixion[4]

4 Reference from DSS (Department of Syriac Studies)

Later, she hears about the Resurrection of the Lord and is filled with joy. Some icons of the Myrrh-Bearers at the Tomb depict Theotokos as one of the Myrrh-Bearers.

Syriac Icon of the Myrrh-Bearers at the Tomb

The icons of the Ascension of Christ also depict her along with the apostles, though she was not physically present.

Syriac Icon of the Ascension of Christ

Tradition tells us that the Virgin Mary was the leader of the apostles during the event of the Descent of the Holy Spirit.

Syriac Icon of the Pentecost

After Pentecost, as Christ had entrusted her to him, St. John the Apostle and Theologian took the Theotokos to Ephesus. He built a house and they lived there. This house is now revered by several Christians worldwide as the *Catholic Shrine of the House of Virgin Mary.*

House of Virgin Mary in Ephesus, Turkey

1. After this, St. John left to preach the Gospel, and Mary left for Jerusalem. St. Gabriel appeared to her and asked what final wishes she had before she departed from this world. She wished that she could join her son in heaven and that she could see her spiritual sons one last time. Wish granted, the twelve apostles, who were scattered across the globe, preaching the good news to

the Gentiles, were miraculously carried to Jerusalem and brought to the aid of the Theotokos. Later, the Holy Virgin fell asleep in Christ, and the twelve apostles, full of grief, buried her in the Garden of Gethsemane, where the Lord prayed with agony before his passion. Church historians debate and dispute over the exact age of the Holy Virgin at her repose. It is estimated to have happened around 50-52 AD.

Syriac Icon of the Dormition of the Virgin[5]

5 Picture courtesy livingmaronite organisation

Unfortunately, St. Thomas, the Apostle, had arrived late. And when he finally arrived 3 days after her demise, he asked his fellow apostles if he could behold her countenance just once more. Permission granted, the twelve headed over to the tomb of the Virgin and opened her coffin. But they couldn't find her body inside! Thinking that someone stole her body, they began to weep. Then suddenly, a radiant light shone upon them, and they looked up to find the heavenly host carrying the Theotokos into the heavens. The Holy Virgin granted St. Thomas her girdle and her face-mantel. These holy relics were then taken to India, and with it, St. Thomas performed many miracles. Church Fathers teach us that the Mother of God was taken up to heaven in both body and spirit, for Christ did not want his mother to experience earthly corruption.

Syriac Icon of the Apostles finding the empty coffin and the Theotokos giving St. Thomas her girdle

The Liturgical Calendar of the Syriac Orthodox Church has 8 feasts dedicated to the Theotokos. They are:

1. The Intercession of the Theotokos for the Seeds - January 15
2. The Annunciation of our Lord to the Theotokos - March 25
3. The Intercession of the Theotokos for the Harvest - May 15
4. The Dormition (Falling-Asleep) of the Theotokos - August 15
5. The Intercession of the Theotokos for the Vine - August 15
6. The Nativity of the Theotokos - September 8 (not a canonical feast)
7. The Entry of the Theotokos into the temple - November 27
8. The Glorification of the Theotokos - December 26.

Chapter Six

Holy Synods

What are synods? Well, synods are meetings of a large group of ecclesiastical hierarchy to decide ecclesiastical affairs. The Church believes in 3 ecumenical synods, which are recorded and commemorated in the 5th Diptych of the Divine Liturgy. They are:

1. Council of Nicea

Orthodox Icon of the Synod of Nicea

Convened by Constantine the Great, this assembly of 318 bishops primarily was gathered to judge the heresy of Arius, which denied that God the Son (our Lord Jesus Christ) was consubstantial with God the Father, but stated that rather, he was the highest creation of the Father. The heresy was condemned by the fathers of the synod. St. Athanasius the Great, pope of Alexandria, who then was a deacon and secretary of his predecessor, St. Alexander, is called the roaring lion of Nicea since he was the leading figure against the heretic Arius. The synod, after condemning Arius, also created a creed, called the Nicene Creed that kept the record of the faith of the Church, and they also decided the yearly date of the Feast of the Resurrection of the Lord (Easter).

2. Council of Constantinople

Orthodox Icon of the Synod of Constantinople

Convened by Theodosius the Great, this assembly of 150 bishops primarily was gathered to judge the heresy of Macedonius, which denied that the Holy Spirit was God. The heresy was condemned by the fathers of the synod. This sentence was also added to the Nicene Creed: "And (we believe) in the one, living, Holy Spirit, the life-giving lord of all, who proceeds from the Father, and who with the Father and the Son is worshipped and glorified, who spoke through the Apostles and Prophets.

3. Council of Ephesus

Icon of the Synod of Ephesus

Convened by Theodosius II, this assembly of 159 bishops was gathered to judge the heresy of Nestorius, which denied that Christ was one person, and taught that Jesus Christ and God the Son were 2 separate persons (with Christ being man and the Son being God), that the Holy Virgin Mary be venerated not as Theotokos (Mother of God), but as Christotokos (Mother of Christ). The heresy was condemned by the fathers of the synod, and the following part: "Was incarnate of the Holy Virgin Mary, Mother of God" was added to the Nicene Creed.

Chapter Seven

Fathers of The Church

The 5th Diptych also holds the record of 29 of the names of some Church fathers they are:

1. St. James, cousin of our Lord and first archbishop of Jerusalem.
2. St. Ignatius the Luminous, patriarch of Antioch and martyr.
3. St. Clement, pope of Rome and martyr.
4. St. Dionysius of Alexandria, pope of Alexandria.
5. St. Athanasius the Great, pope of Alexandria.
6. St. Julius, pope of Rome.
7. St. Basil the Great, archbishop of Caesarea.
8. St. Gregory the Theologian, patriarch of Constantinople / St. Gregory, brother of St. Basil and bishop of Nyssa.
9. St. Dioscorus, pope of Alexandria.

10. St. Timothy the Great, pope of Alexandria.
11. St. Philoxenus, bishop of Mabbug and martyr.
12. St. Anthimus, patriarch of Constantinople.
13. St. John Chrysostom, patriarch of Constantinople and confessor.
14. St. Cyril, pope of Alexandria.
15. St. Severus, patriarch of Antioch.
16. St. Jacob Baradeus, bishop of Edessa.
17. St. Ephrem the Syrian, deacon, doctor, and hymnographer.
18. St. Jacob, bishop of Batnan in Serugh and doctor / St. Jacob, bishop of Edessa.
19. St. Isaac the Syrian, bishop of Nineveh, doctor, and ascetic.
20. St. Balay, bishop of Balsh.
21. St. Barsawmo, ascetic, bishop of Nisibis and chief of the Mourners.
22. St. Simeon Stylites, ascetic.
23. St. Abahay, bishop of Mardin.
24. St. Ignatius Elias III, patriarch of Antioch.

25. St. Baselius Yeldo, catholicos.
26. St. Gregorius of Parumala, bishop of Niranam and Thumpamon.
27. St. Gregorius Abdul Jaleel, archbishop of Jerusalem.
28. St. Osthatheus Sleebo, bishop of Mosul.
29. St. Athanasius Paulose, bishop of Aluva and protector of the True Faith.
30. St. Coorilos Euyakim, archbishop of Malankara.
31. St. Baselius Shakrallah, catholicos.

Chapter Eight

Clergy

The Syriac Orthodox Church has several ranks of shepherds to aid the faithful congregation in their spiritual life. These are the clergy of the Patriarchate of Antioch:

The Patriarch is the Supreme Head of the Church, second to the Lord. St. Peter the Apostle is believed to be the first Patriarch, who established the Apostolic Throne of St. Peter in Antioch, as it is known today. The Patriarchs oversees the entire universal Church and favour and assist the faithful congregation. The current patriarch is His Holiness Mor Ignatius Aphrem II.

H.H. Mor Ignatius Aphrem II

The Catholicos (Maphrian/Maphryono) is Head of Most of the Churches, second to the Patriarch. H.B. Mor Baselios Thomas I is the current Catholicos.

H.B. Mor Baselios Thomas

Bishops oversee small regions of churches and cathedrals called dioceses. The term bishop comes from the Greek episkopos, which means overseer. When bishops visit other dioceses, they dress in black so that people recognise the diocesan bishop, who will be dressed in red. In the presence of the Patriarch, bishops never wear red. There is another rank for bishops, a superior one, archbishop (metropolitan), an overseer of an archdiocese (which is a really big diocese).

H.E. Mor Dionysius John Kawak,
Archbishop of the Eastern United States[6]

Priests oversee individual churches (parishes) and act as shepherds to the members of the Church, offering the Holy Mysteries and helping them in their spiritual life. Monks can also be ordained priests, and when they are, they are called hieromonks. Syriac Orthodox Priests in Syria, Damascus, Lebanon, and places like that wear a round-shaped, black, priestly hat called the f'iro and only use the cylindrical f'iro for non-liturgical affairs.

6 Picture Courtesy malankara.com

Late Fr. George Cacan.

Rev. Fr. Gheevarghese Vazhattil, my grandfather.

Syriac Orthodox Priests in Malankara wear a cylindrical, black f'iro for every affair, be it liturgical and non-liturgical.

Deacons assist the priest during Church services. Deacons are divided into 7 ranks.

1. The Hymnist (M'zam'rono) leads the congregation in the singing of hymns.

2. The Reader (Q'oruyo) reads the readings for the day during the services.

3. The Subdeacon (Afud'yaq'no) are deacons who are about to complete their service as deacons. In earlier times, they were also assigned to shut the Church doors at the beginning of the Liturgy of the Faithful.

4. The Full-Deacon (M'sham'shono) has completed his service as a deacon and is about to be ordained a priest. It is usually a full-deacon who assists the priest during the Liturgy.

5. The Archdeacon (Arkadyaq'no) is the leader of deacons.

Nuns are women who leave their past sinful lives and accept Christ. They live in convents, mostly found in Kothamangalam, Puthencruz, and Syria.

Monks are men who leave their past sinful lives and accept Christ, very similar to nuns, though they are male. They live in monasteries.

Altar Assistants are those who assist the celebrant in the celebration of the Eucharist when deacons are not present or are fewer.

Altar Assistant Joey Akman of St. Mary's Syriac Orthodox Church

Chapter Nine

Structure of The Church Building

A Model Syriac Orthodox Church or Cathedral is divided into 3 parts: The sanctuary, the chancel, and the nave.

The Sanctuary (Mad'baho) is the place that holds the Altar. It is located in the eastern part of the Church. This is where the bishop/priest, the deacons, and the altar assistants celebrate the Divine Liturgy.

Sanctuary of the Monastery of St. Moses the Abyssinian (Day'ro d' Mor Mushe Q'osuyo)

The Chancel (Qest'rumo) is the place where the celebrants perform the Church services, other than the Divine Liturgy, and where the children stand during the Divine Liturgy (in some churches). In some churches, the choir also stands here. The chancel is disconnected from the sanctuary with a large veil. In most churches, the baptistery (where converts are baptised) is located in the Chancel.

Chancel of St. Peter's Syriac Orthodox Church

The Nave is the place where the faithful congregation/ recipient stands during the Church services.

Nave of Syriac Orthodox Church of the Forty Martyrs

Chapter Ten

Holy Mysteries

The Syriac Orthodox Church has 7 mysteries inherited from Apostolic Tradition. They are the Holy Eucharist, Holy Baptism, Holy Confirmation, Holy Matrimony, Holy Priesthood, Holy Unction, and Holy Confession.

The Holy Eucharist (Q'urobo/Q'urbono) is a mystery that Christ himself introduced. Look at St. Matthew 26: 26-29. We also read in St. John 6: 26-51 that even before the Last Supper, the Lord had spoken about the mystery of the Eucharist. The Holy Eucharist fulfils the sanctity of the other mysteries, thus achieving the honorific title: *'Queen of the Mysteries'*. What is it? Well, the Eucharist is the holy and glorious body and blood of Christ our Lord, which he entrusted the apostles to celebrate. The apostles, obeying the command of the Saviour, have celebrated the divine mystery, handing this responsibility down to their successors, the modern-day clergy. When we partake of the Eucharist, Christ, as he taught, abides in us and we in him. The Eucharistic Bread (Host), offered every mass, always contains a small portion of the bread that the Lord used at the Last Supper. The general Eucharistic rite or Anaphora, as it is called, is the book of the rite of the celebration of the Eucharist. In Syriac, it is known as *Teq'so*. There are almost 80 *Teq'se* in use, but the *Teq'so* written by St. James, cousin of our Lord is the one used on most Sundays. The Teq'so of St. James alone is to be used for the celebration of the Eucharist on *Moronoyo* (relating to the Lord) feast days. However, there are almost 80 other *Teq'se*, for example, one of St. John Chrysostom, one of St. Basil the Great, one of St. Jacob Baradaeus, one of St. Dionysius Jacob Bar Slibi. The pattern in which the celebrant breaks the Eucharistic bread differs according to the current liturgical season. From the feast of *Q'udosh Id'to* (the Sanctification of the Church) until the Feast of the Resurrection (Easter), and also on the Thursday of the Mysteries (Great/Maundy Thursday) and the Saturday of the Lights (Great/Black Saturday), the bread is broken in the likeness of a lamb. However, from the Feast of the Resurrection until the feast of the Elevation of the Cross, the bread is broken in the likeness of a child. And from the feast of the Elevation of the Cross until the feast of *Q'udosh Id'to*, the bread is broken in the likeness of a cross.

Syriac Icon of the Communion of the Apostles[7]

The Holy Baptism (Mam'odeetho) is a mystery that began before the commencement of Christ's Ministry. St. John the Forerunner (Baptist), after dwelling in the wilderness for so long, began to baptise in the River Jordan. Christ did partake of his cousin, St. John's Baptism. The Lord himself did baptise as well, though

7 Reference from DSS (Department of Syriac Studies)

it was not him who baptised but his apostles (St. John 3:26, 4:1-2). As his ascension draws near, he commands his Apostles to **'go therefore and make disciples of all the nations, baptising them in the name of the Father and of the Son and of the Holy Spirit'** (St. Matthew 28:19). What is baptism, you may ask. Well, after a short period after a child is born (if the child's parents are members of the Church and believers), he or she is brought to his or her parish, and the services of the holy mystery of baptism begin. In the service, he or she is immersed in a mixture of hot and cold water and the Holy Chrism. This mystery signifies us dying to our sins, and our spirit being renewed by Christ, through his sacrifice on the cross, thus making us his children. Let me explain further. During the service, the celebrant pours half a vessel of cold water and half a vessel of hot water, crossing his arms, into the baptismal font. Then, during the prayers and rituals, he sprinkles a drop of the Holy Chrism each in both the eastern and western parts of the baptismal font. Then he crosses his arms once more and pours 2 drops in the southern and northern parts. Then, finally, the child is immersed in the baptismal font, while prayers are said out loud. Though most of the Church is familiar with baptising infants, mature men and women can also be baptised into the faith. The procedures differ, as the person to be baptised bends over the baptismal font in silent reverence, as the celebrant pours the mixture over his or her head. If the infant to be baptised needs to be taken to the hospital immediately, an archdeacon (a chief of the deacons) baptises him or her in a very fast procedure. The child's paternal grandparents are called godparents, and the celebrant makes them promise that they will raise the child in the faith of the Church. The Church only allows a person to be baptised once, since the physical birth is once, so is the spiritual re-birth. This is all about the mystery of the Holy Baptism.

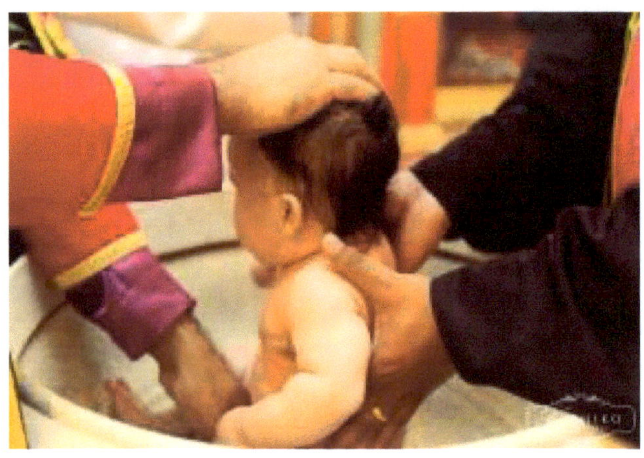

Baptism Service at St. Mary's Syrian Orthodox Church

The Holy Confirmation (M'uron) is a mystery performed immediately after another mystery, that is, the mystery of the Holy Baptism. The infant/mature man or woman receives the flairs and fruits of the Holy Spirit and is established in the belief of the Church, thus commencing their growth in their devout vigour, and is acknowledged as a Christian associate inside the patriarchate. St. Dionysius Jacob Bar Salibi (Died: 1171) quotes that "we see a reference to the Holy Chrism in the Old Testament, particularly the reading from Exodus 30:23-27, 31-33. In the New Testament, the apostles would rest their hands on new believers and bless them. This 'laying of hands' was the entire service of the confirmation of a Christian believer and is mentioned twice by St. Luke the Evangelist in the Book of the Acts of the Apostles. The first time is Acts 8:17 and the second one is Acts 19:6. But it was simply hopeless for the Apostles that they rest their hands on every Christian. Thus, they advised the ritual of consecration with the oil of the Holy Chrism, in place of the custom of the laying of hands, as St. John the Apostle writes in his first epistle (1 St. John 2:20-21). We can also find the prescription of the use of consecration in 2 of the Pauline Epistles.

This is 2 Corinthians 1:21, 22 and Ephesians 4:30. Now, who gets to consecrate with the Holy Chrism? Priests collected their divine consent and assignment from Christ our Lord, whom St. Paul calls a priest himself (Hebrews 6:20). Also, priests likewise collected their authorisation to consecrate with the Chrism from bishops, who received it from the Apostles (Acts 8:17). Now, the Holy Chrism is not only used for consecrating new believers. It is used for consecrating churches, cathedrals, chapels, altars, and the Tab'litho (Tablet) of each place of worship. Now, how vital is the Divine Chrism? Basically, it is crucial for the redemption of humanity. The Mystery of Holy Baptism is illegal and imperfect without the Mystery of Holy Confirmation. We can prove this by pointing out that the Mystery of Baptism renews our spirit and makes it ready for the advent of the Holy Spirit. However, the Holy Spirit has not yet come. Then, the Mystery of Confirmation fills the renewed spirit with the fruits and gifts of the Holy Spirit, thus sealing the spirit with the grace of the Holy Spirit. A demonstration of this statement is in the Book of the Acts of the Apostles: Acts 8:14-17. The Patriarch and the Maphrian (Catholicos), who are the leading hierarchs of the Church, are the 2 people permitted to compose the oil of confirmation, as the Lord instructed the Prophet Moses. New believers (including newly baptised mature men and women) are consecrated after their baptism, and it is made once a year because the Crucifixion and Resurrection of the Lord were once. The Holy Chrism is made every year on the Thursday of the Mysteries because it is the eve of the Friday of the Crucifixion and so that it may be accessible on the Sunday of the Resurrection for the newly baptised members of the Church. Believers are granted the Mystery of Confirmation only once they're baptised. Then, immediately after the newly baptised believer is anointed with the Chrism, he or she receives the Holy Eucharist. The Holy Chrism is composed of about 40 ingredients.

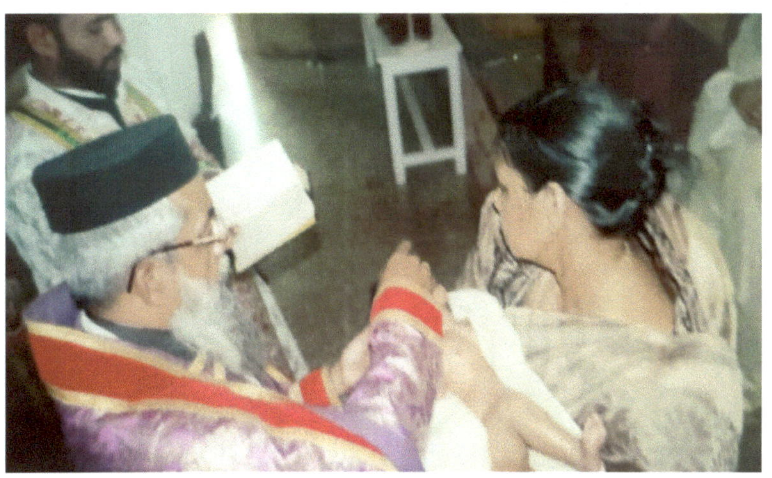

My sister, Hannah Raichel's confirmation service.

The Holy Priesthood (Koh'nutho) is one of the most important mysteries in the Church. Though all the faithful have a role in the royal priesthood (1 St. Peter 2:9), priests have a special role. The responsibilities of all Syriac Orthodox priests are carrying out the mysteries, managing parish issues, explaining church doctrine, and advising and directing the believers to redemption. St. Paul the Apostle calls Christ a high priest himself, and all priests inherit their authority to carry out the Mysteries and other church services from him.

Late Fr. George Cacan

The Holy Matrimony is the mystery of the union of one man and one woman in love. However, this mystery is not compulsory for all the believers of the Church. The Lord established this mystery at the very beginning of mankind when he created a wife for Adam, Eve, out of his own rib. It is also written in Genesis 2:24: "Therefore a man shall leave his father and mother and be joined to his wife, and they shall become one flesh." The holy matrimony is to be solely of one man and one woman.

Coptic Icon of Ten Biblical Marriages

The Holy Unction (also known as the Anointing of the Sick) is the Mystery of Healing. Christ our God was indeed a healer, as mentioned in the Gospel several times. According to the New Testament, bodily illnesses were caused by the illness of the soul. The souls tainted with sinful stains were attacked by diseases of all kinds.

An incredible story of Christ healing the sick is found in St. Mark 2:3-12, in which the Lord forgives and heals a paralytic lowered into the building through the roof. Another time, as described in St. Matthew 17:14-20, the Twelve attempted to heal an epileptic but failed. Then, Christ came along and cured the person completely, and upon inquiry, he said that they weren't able to cast the demon out of the possessed because of their scepticism. Thus, faith is needed for the sick to be healed. Later, the Lord granted his apostles the power to cast out demons, purify lepers, resurrect the departed, and most importantly, cure the ailing (St. Matthew 10:8). St. Mark the Evangelist also mentions in his Gospel that the apostles also freed the possessed and, by smearing with oil, cured many (St. Mark 6:13). From all these demonstrations, we understand that Christ established the mystery of unction himself from the very start. The apostles also approve of this. St. James, cousin of our Lord, writes in his epistle, "Is anyone among you sick? Let him call for the elders of the Church, and let them pray over him, anointing him with oil in the name of the Lord. And the prayer of faith will save the sick, and the Lord will raise him up. And if he has committed sins, he will be forgiven" (St. James 5:14, 15). We shouldn't confuse the oil used in the mystery of Unction with the Holy Chrism. The oil grants the ill believer strength to undertake his or her disease and the Tempter.

The Holy Repentance is the last of the Holy Mysteries of the Church. It is mentioned by St. John the Apostle in his Gospel (St. John 20:22-23). Our Lord gave authority to his apostles and their successors, the clergy today, that they may absolve the sins of the laypeople. The penitent is to think of the sin which he or she committed and ponder them, then go to the priest and confess each and every sin remembered. It is sinful to conceal any sins in mind, and the penitent must honestly repent with a sense of regret. It is improper to regret past sins after the completion of the holy mystery since that would be denying the truth in the absolution. After confessing sins, the penitent shall accept the canonical penalty given by the priest. These are some general exhortations for the priest.

1. The priest shall be well aware of and familiar with the heavenly and ecclesiastical rules to ascertain if the penitent is worthy of absolution. After this, the priest, like a spiritual doctor, is to care for the health of the penitent's soul.

2. Like the penitent, who is to reveal all known sins to the priest, the priest is to conceal all confessed sins of the penitent until death. In the same way, the penitent is to conceal the priest's advice until death.

3. If a penitent asks a priest for the celebration of the mystery, the priest should never refuse the request

and be always ready to answer the call and to honestly implore the Lord to help him complete his service properly and reverently.

4. The mystery is to be celebrated at a church alone. The priest is to wear a stole around his neck, and he is to sit on a chair, which is to be placed in a special position in the church building, so that he be noticed immediately by the laypeople upon entry into the church. However, if the penitent is not able to come to Church, due to ill health or any other issue, the priest is permitted to go to the penitent's house. When the penitent confesses his or her sins, the priest is to sit in a special place, where he is seen by all those present.

5. If the priest discovers that the penitent is unaware and unfamiliar with the truth and doctrine of the Holy Church, then he is to attempt enlightening and teaching the true faith at the time when the mystery is celebrated, but if not possible, he is to attempt at a more convenient time.

6. If, due to extreme ailment or any other hindrance, the penitent is not able to speak and can use sign language for confessing sins alone, the priest is to grant the individual absolution.

Chapter Eleven

Saints

The saints are fellow Christians who achieved sanctity and holiness through piety, faith, and righteousness. The saints have fallen asleep in the Lord and now rejoice in His company in heaven. The Holy Virgin Mary, the Mother of God, is known as the queen of the saints. There are different ranks of saints.

There has been a lot of opposition to the veneration and intercession of saints, especially among Protestants. Saints are alive in Christ. If any Christian dies, not only the saints, (s)he still lives in Christ. The saints hear us in the Holy Spirit, and they pray with us and for us. Yes, our Lord is the sole mediator for us to God the Father (1 St. Timothy 2:5). But the saints are the great cloud of witnesses who pray with us (Hebrews 12:1). Let us also pay attention to what the Apostle St. Peter says in his first epistle (3:12), "For the eyes of the LORD are on the righteous, and His ears are open to their prayers; but the face of the LORD is against those who do evil." And what St. James says in his epistle (5:16), "The effective, fervent prayer of a righteous man avails much."

1. **Martyrs** are those saints who have publicly professed their faith in the Most Holy Trinity and have therefore been killed. Christians attaining martyrdom during the rule of Emperors Nero, Trajan, Diocletian, and Maximian was common, as these vile rulers unleashed persecution upon the Church. The reign of Diocletian, from 283 AD, is known as the age of martyrs. The first of the martyrs was St. Stephen, who, upon professing his faith before the council of the Sanhedrin, was stoned to death outside Jerusalem by a crowd of Jews (Acts 5-7).

2. **Ascetics**, who were monks and nuns, sometimes hermits and hermitesses, dedicated their lives to living alone and being loyal to the Lord alone. Common among them are Sts. Anthony and Paul of Thebes, the fathers of Christian monasticism.

3. **Hierarchs**, who defended the true faith against heresies and worked works of piety and righteousness. Well-known among them is St. John Chrysostom, who was an ardent speaker and the Archbishop of Constantinople.

4. **Prophets and Prophetesses**, who prophesied and spoke the word of God which was told them in visions and dreams. Prophethood was common among the Israelites in the Old Testament Times. Two public favourites among them were St. Moses and St. Elijah, the first known for his leadership in the return from slavery in Egypt, and the second for his fiery miracles. An example for a prophetess in the Old Testament is St. Deborah.

5. **Apostles**, who are those special twelve disciples whom our Lord himself chose for preaching the Gospel throughout the world. All of them except St. John were martyred. St. Peter and St. Paul were the chiefs of the apostles.

6. **Evangelists**, who wrote about the nativity, life, sayings, death, and resurrection of our Lord, so that the future generations of the Church could know about it.

7. **Emissaries**, who, other than the apostles, preached the Gospel. The 72 Emissaries were also picked by our Lord (St. Luke 10:1), however, they were not numbered with the apostles. Other missionaries can be counted with them.

8. **Pious Royals**, who were faithful and devout Christian rulers, built churches and monasteries, and also convened synods to protect the True Faith.

One of them is St. Constantine the Great, the first-ever Christian emperor who believed and was baptised, and who also convened the Council of Nicea and funded the discovery of the Holy Cross.

Chapter Twelve

The Chronological List of Our Patriarchs

In AD 37, St. Peter the Apostle established the Holy See in Syrian Antioch. This was because Antioch was open to the Church, and the believers here had earlier been nicknamed Christians (Acts 11:26). Therefore, our Church is true and apostolic because St. Peter was our first patriarch. This is the list of his successors.

1. St. Peter the Apostle.
2. St. Evodius the Emissary.
3. St. Ignatius the Illuminator.
4. St. Heron I of Antioch.
5. St. Cornelius of Antioch.
6. St. Heron II of Antioch.
7. St. Theophilus of Antioch.
8. St. Maximus I of Antioch.

9. St. Serapion of Antioch.
10. St. Ascelpiades the Confessor.
11. Mor Philetus.
12. Mor Zebinnus.
13. St. Babylas the Martyr.
14. Mor Fabius.
15. St. Demetrius.
16. Mor Paul I of Samosate.
17. Mor Domnus I.
18. Mor Timaeus.
19. Mor Cyril I.
20. Mor Tyrannion.
21. Mor Vitalis.
22. St. Philogonius.
23. Mor Paulinus of Tyre.
24. St. Eustathius the Great.

Then, the Arian heretics took over the Holy See and named these Patriarchs:

Eulalius.

Euphronius.

Flacillus.

Stephen I.

Leontius.

Eudoxius, and

Euzoius.

Then everything was made right, and the canonical patriarch was renamed. However, there was still an Arian patriarch, who will not be mentioned anymore.

25. Mor Meletius
26. St. Flavian I.
27. Mor Porphyrus.
28. Mor Alexander.
29. Mor Theodotus.
30. Mor John I.
31. Mor Domnus II.
32. Maximus II.

Then patriarch Maximus renounced the true faith, and due to him, the Chalcedonians took over the Holy See and named these heretical Patriarchs.

Basil and

Acacius.

Then everything was made right again, and these patriarchs were named.

33. Mor Martyrius.

34. Mor Peter II the Fuller.

35. Mor Bladius.

36. Mor Flavian II.

37. St. Severus the Great.

Then the Chalcedonians, after sending Patriarch St. Severus to exile, took over again in AD 518 and named these heretical patriarchs, whose line continues the Antiochian Orthodox Church.

Paul the Jew.

Euphrosius, and

Ephrem of Amid.

Six years passed, after Patriarch St. Severus had reposed, and finally, another patriarch was named.

38. Mor Sergius of Tella.

    The Holy See remained without a patriarch for another 4 years. Finally another Patriarch was named.

39. Paul II the Black of Alexandria.

    In AD 575, Patriarch Paul II renounced the true faith and joined the Chalcedonians, therefore the Holy See deposed him and remained without a Patriarch for the next few years. Then another Patriarch was named.

40. Mor Peter III of Raqqa.
41. Mor Julian I.
42. Mor Athanasius I Gammolo.
43. St. John II of the Sedre.
44. Mor Theodore.
45. Mor Severus II Bar Masqeh.
46. Mor Athanasius II.
47. Mor Julian II.
48. Mor Elias I.
49. Mor Athanasius III.

50. Mor Iwanis I.

    After Patriarch Mor Iwanis reposed, 2 patriarchs were named according to the wish of the Caliph.

    Euwanis I, and

    Athanasius Sandalaya.

    Then, more canonical Patriarchs were named.

51. Mor George I.
52. Mor Joseph.
53. St. Cyriacus of Tigrit.
54. Mor Dionysius I of Tellmahreh.
55. Mor John III.
56. Mor Ignatius II.
57. Mor Theodosius Romanus of Tigrit.
58. Mor Dionysius II.
59. Mor John IV Qurzahli.
60. Mor Basil I.
61. Mor John V.
62. Mor Iwanis II.
63. Mor Dionysius III.

64. Mor Abraham I.

65. Mor John VI Sarigta.

66. Mor Athanasius IV of Salah.

67. Mor John VII Bar Abdoun.

68. Mor Dionysius IV Yahyo.

    Again, because of internal quarrels within the Church, the Holy See remained without a Patriarch for the next few years. But later, the Patriarch was named.

69. Mor John VIII.

70. Mor Athanasius V.

71. Mor John IX Bar Susan.

72. Mor Basil II.

    Then, after Patriarch Mor Basil II reposed, another John Bar Abdoun had himself named Patriarch and made trouble in the Church. The Holy See deposed him, but he made trouble until AD 1091.

73. Mor Dionysius V Lazarus.

74. Mor Iwanis III.

75. Mor Dionysius VI.

76. Mor Athanasius VI Bar Khamoro.

77. Mor John X Bar Mawdyono.
78. Mor Athanasius VII Bar Qutreh.
79. St. Michael the Great.
80. Mor Athanasius VIII.
81. Mor John XI.
82. Mor Ignatius III David.
83. Mor John XII Bar Ma'dani.
84. Mor Ignatius IV Yeshu.
85. Mor Philoxenus I Nemrud.
86. Mor Michael II.
87. Mor Michael III Yeshu.
88. Mor Basil III Gabriel.
89. Mor Philoxenus II the Writer.
90. Mor Basil IV Shem'un.
91. Mor Ignatius Behnam Al-Hadii.
92. Mor Ignatius Khalaf.
93. Mor Ignatius John XIII.
94. Mor Ignatius Nuh of Lebanon.
95. Mor Ignatius Yeshu I.

96. Mor Ignatius Jacob I.
97. Mor Ignatius David I.
98. Mor Ignatius Abd-Allah I.
99. Mor Ignatius Ne'met Allah I.
100. Mor Ignatius David II Shah.
101. Mor Ignatius Pilate I.
102. St. Ignatius Hidayat Aloho (popularly called St. Ahatallah.)
103. Mor Ignatius Simon I.
104. Mor Ignatius Yeshu II Qamsheh.
105. Mor Ignatius Abdul Masih I.
106. Mor Ignatius George II.
107. Mor Ignatius Isaac Azar.
108. Mor Ignatius Shukr Allah II.
109. Mor Ignatius George III.
110. Mor Ignatius George IV.
111. Mor Ignatius Matthew.
112. Mor Ignatius Yunan.
113. Mor Ignatius George V.

114. Mor Ignatius Elias II.

115. Mor Ignatius Jacob II.

116. Mor Ignatius Peter IV.

117. Ignatius Abdul Masih II.

    The Holy See deposed Patriarch Abdul Masih II in 1905.

118. Mor Ignatius Abd-Allah II.

119. St. Ignatius Elias III.

120. Mor Ignatius Aphrem I Barsoum.

121. Mor Ignatius Jacob III.

122. Mor Ignatius Zakka I Iwas.

123. Mor Ignatius Aphrem II.

    To this day, Patriarch Mor Aphrem II oversees the Holy See and occupies the Apostolic Throne of St. Peter.

Chapter Thirteen

The General History of The Holy Church

After the ascension of our Lord and the descent of the Holy Spirit on Pentecost, the Church commenced in Jerusalem. St. James, cousin of our Lord, was chosen and named the archbishop of Jerusalem. As we read in Acts 5-7, the Hellenistic converts complained that the Church did not tend to their poor widows and orphans. Therefore, the apostles chose 7 men from among the believers, who were full of the Holy Spirit and faith, led by St. Stephen. Later, due to the great preaching of the archdeacon, the Jews arose against him and gathered a mob, and they stoned him to death. We read in Acts 11 that the Church was scattered across the lands of the Gentiles after that tremendous incident. All the believers except the apostles fled Jerusalem. They were to preach to Jews alone. But the Gentile converts began preaching to the Antiochians, and many souls were won. Therefore, the Church prospered in Syrian Antioch (also called Antioch-on-the-Orontes), and tidings of this came to the apostles in Jerusalem. Therefore, they sent St. Barnabas to them, and he was wonderstruck and strengthened them in the faith, encouraging them to continue as they were. Finally, he left for Tarsus and found the newly baptised St. Paul, who had just joined the group of the apostles. From there, St. Paul accompanied him back to Antioch, and they taught and strengthened the Church there for some years. Later they were joined by St. Peter, who established the Holy See there in AD 37. Later, through the mission of St. Thomas, who came to India in AD 52, the Church spread to here as well. After the martyrdom of the apostles and the repose of St. John, the Church suffered under the Emperors Nero, Trajan, Diocletian, and Maximian. The most violent period of persecution began with the beginning of Diocletian's reign, in AD 283/284. This early period of the Church is called the age of martyrs.

Later, when St. Constantine came into reign and issued the Edict of Milan in AD 313, the Church was freed. But there was still the invasion of heretics.

When the heresy of Arius arose, St. Constantine convened the Council of Nicea in AD 325. Here, the fathers condemned Arius and his followers and decided when the Feast of the Resurrection should be celebrated. It was now that 4 important archdioceses, which were prominent Christian centres, were recognised as patriarchates. These were the 4 archdioceses of

Antioch, Alexandria, Rome, and the newly founded Constantinople. Its archbishops would be called patriarchs, or as the Latin equivalent, popes. The 4 patriarchs would be the fathers of fathers and overseers of the universal Church. Among these, the Holy See of Antioch was given a superior position. The archdiocese of Jerusalem and its archbishop was also honoured with a high position in the ecclesiastical hierarchy.

In 381 AD, Emperor Theodosius the Great convened the Council of Constantinople, to debate the heresy of Macedonianism. The doctrine was condemned. In 431 AD, Emperor Theodosius II convened the Council of Ephesus, to debate the heresy of Nestorianism. Nestorius, the patriarch of Constantinople, had espoused a heresy that Jesus Christ and God the Son were 2 different persons, and that the Son only dwelt in Christ. Some of the major combatants of Nestorianism were St. Cyril, pope of Alexandria, and Mor Celestine, pope of Rome. The council's decision was rejected by many Assyrians, who broke away from the Holy Church and accepted Nestorianism.

Later, a second council was convened at Ephesus in 449 AD. This was to debate the heresy of Eutychianism. Eutyches, an abbot from Constantinople, espoused that Christ had one incarnate nature, but that his divinity consumed his humanity. Many of the fathers rejected it. But a few accepted the heresy. Leo, pope of Rome, could not attend the council, but he sent his representatives with a tome written by his hand, the Tome of Leo, which authorised and defended the heresy. Therefore, the council was a failure.

Then the biggest schism that divided the Church happened. At the Council of Chalcedon in AD 451, convened by Emperor Marcian, St. Dioscorus, pope of Alexandria, opposed Leo, pope of Rome, to his face when he preached that Christ had 2 natures. The emperor had St. Dioscorus punished. The other bishops were afraid, and they signed the decrees of the council, accepting the heresy of Dyophysitism. Then St. Dioscorus wrote under the document, stating that he excommunicated all those who signed the decrees. Sts. Dioscorus, Macarius (bishop of Edko), Timothy (the Great), and Philoxenus (bishop of Mabbug) were exiled to Gangra. St. Dioscorus reposed, and St. Philoxenus was suffocated and martyred. St. Macarius returned to Alexandria and was martyred there. Then, the Sees of Rome and Constantinople schismated and broke away from the true faith, accepting the heresy of Dyophysitism. Meanwhile, the Holy Sees of Antioch and Alexandria remained firm in the true faith. The Dyophysites waged war on the True Church, as Syrian and Coptic bishops were exiled and even martyred. St. Severus, patriarch of Antioch, was exiled to Egypt. The patriarchate was forced to move from Antioch to various locations.

Then, there came a crucial time when only 3 bishops remained. However, the Lord raised and strengthened his Church through his servant, St. Jacob Baradaeus. St. Jacob was born in Tall Mawzalt in AD 500. Later, he travelled to Constantinople to meet the empress and wife of Emperor Justinian, St. Theodora. Through her influence, she managed to get him ordained as the Bishop of Edessa. Then he travelled across the globe, ordaining the Patriarchs of Antioch and Alexandria, 27 bishops, and hundreds of priests and deacons.

After various movements, the Patriarchate settled in the Dayro d-Mor Hananyo in AD 1106. The Church continued to suffer under the Arabs, the Mongols, the Crusaders, the Mamluks, and the Ottomans.

The great Patriarchs of the Church, such as Sts. Severus and Michael the Great, shepherded and contributed to the Church. They authored treatises and prayers to be included in the Church. Some of St. Severus' great works are the manitho sung at the public commencement of the Holy *Q'urbono* and the final prayer of the *sh'himo* Compline (*soutoro*). One of St. Michael's great works is his Chronicle, recording world history.

The year of 1915 is known as the year of *Sayfo*, or the sword. The Turks unleashed a terrible genocide, and a quarter million of the faithful were martyred. They are honoured as saints on June 15.

Here is a short introduction to the history of the Holy Church in Malankara.

After the coming of Vasco Da Gama to India in AD 1498, the Portuguese set up colonies in Malankara and began to forcefully bring the Syriac Orthodox faithful there into the subjection of the Roman Pope. The Roman Catholic Archbishop of Goa, Menezes, asked the aid of the local rulers and, in June of AD 1599, convened the Council of Diamper, forcibly bringing the yoke of the Roman Pope upon the Syriac Orthodox faithful. Later, he travelled to the many Syriac Orthodox churches and monasteries and converted them into the Catholic faith, and even took to burn the important Syriac Orthodox books and manuscripts holding the history of the Church in Malankara. At first, many among the faithful willingly became subjects of the Roman Pope, but the vast majority refused. They sent word to the Patriarch of Antioch, asking for a bishop to guide them. Later on, Patriarch St. Ignatius Hidayat Aloho travelled to Malankara in 1653 AD. He reached Surat of Northern India. Immediately upon his arrival, the Portuguese arrested him and took him under their custody to Madras. As St. Hidayat Aloho was in prison at Mylapore, Deacon Itty of Chenganoor and Deacon Kurien of Kurivilaangadu met him. The 2 deacons had come there as pilgrims to the tomb of St. Thomas the Apostle. St. Hidayat Aloho asked them the situation of the Church in Malankara, and upon hearing their grave answer, sent them back to Malankara as his patriarchal envoys, with a stathicon, declaring Archdeacon Thomas as the temporary Archbishop of Malankara, on the condition that proper ordination be given as soon as possible. The Archdeacon Thomas of the Pakalomattom family was elected to the office of archdeacon, as the successor of his uncle, the archdeacon George. He was the leader of the Church in Malankara, due to the absence of a bishop. According to the *sthaticon*, twelve priests gathered together and laid hands on the archdeacon, proclaiming him Archbishop of Malankara. However, the episcopal rights would only be granted after proper ordination. After deacons Itty and Kurien left Mylapore, the Portuguese took St. Hidayat Aloho and put him on a ship leaving for Europe. Many assume it was for his official trial.The Portuguese, who were unable to pronounce the patriarch's Syriac name, simply called him Ahatallah. The saint is still remembered by this name today. Holy tradition state that, on the way to Europe, the Portuguese took hold of St. Hidayat Aloho, tied a heavy stone to him, and drowned him in the ocean. The holy patriarch died a martyr. News of the martyrdom of St. Hidayat Aloho came to the Church in Malankara. The remaining faithful were rightfully enraged at the Portuguese for this atrocity. In their anger and despair, they gathered together at Mattanchery, in January of 1653 AD (the 23rd of Makarom in the Malayalam calendar.) There, they tied a rope to a tall cross of granite, and all who were present took hold of the rope and tugged on it, led by the leaders of the Church in Malankara, and swore an oath to always be subject to the Holy See of Antioch and renounce the Roman Pope and the Jesuit bishops. Thus, the Church in Malankara threw off the yoke of the Roman Pope and requested help from the Holy See. They also recognised archdeacon Thomas as their bishop and organised a four-member advisory council for him, including his friend, Fr. Anjilimootil Itty Thommen. The Portuguese Jesuits had lost the trust of the Church and were forced to flee. However, the Carmelites returned for missionary work, under the order of Pope Alexander VII. The Church also lost the treacherous priests, Fr. Kadavil Chandy and Fr. Parambil Chandy, who accepted the heretical Catholic faith. The prayers of the Church in Malankara were answered when, in 1665 AD, St. Gregorius Abdul Jaleel, the archbishop of Jerusalem, came to Malankara. He arrived at Ponnani in Northern Kerala and then came to St. Thomas Church, in Northern Paravur. He ordained archdeacon Thomas the archbishop of Malankara, with the episcopal name Mor Thomas I. The 2 bishops travelled throughout the land strengthening the true faith.

Soon, the office of the archbishop of Malankara became great. He was called by the name of the Malankara Metropolitan.

In 1876 AD, Mor Peter III, patriarch of Antioch, came to Malankara and convened a holy synod at the Marthoman Church in Mulanthuruthy. This synod is called the Synod (Council) of Mulanthuruthy. Among those present was Mor Dionysius II, of the Pulikot family, and St. Gregorius of Parumala, who was then a monk.

By the early 1910s AD, Mor Dionysius VI, who was the archbishop of Malankara at that time, renounced the true faith. He renounced the supreme authority of the Holy See and preached a new apostolic see of St. Thomas the Apostle. If one were to search through historical records, there is no evidence for an episcopal see established by St. Thomas. It is known that the apostle ordained priests and deacons, but, unlike St. Peter, St. Thomas never ordained an episcopal successor for himself. It was Mor John of Persia, a Syriac bishop under the jurisdiction of the Holy See of Antioch, who signed the decrees of the Council of Nicea (325 AD) for the Church in Malankara. It was bishops sent by the Holy See of Antioch who ordained priests and deacons to serve in Malankara. Anyways, this claim of the archbishop Dionysius VI gained him followers, and with the help of the deposed Patriarch Abdul

Masih II, he began a new catholicate, under the name *The Orthodox Catholicate in Malabar*. At the request of Lord Irwin, the British viceroy of India, St. Ignatius Elias III, patriarch of Antioch, came to Malankara to heal the schism. Despite all his effort and hard work, he failed; and he reposed in Malankara. His holy relics were interred at Manjinikkara Dayro (Abbey.) After a brief reunification in the 1950s, Catholicos Mor Baselius Augen I schismated again. Then, Mor Jacob III, patriarch of Antioch, excommunicated the schismatic faction. This new faction was formed and established rights on the churches and monasteries.

Conclusion

The holy Syriac Orthodox Apostolic See of Antioch and all the East is indigenous and beautiful in her entirety. With her apostolic origin and her preservation of the true faith of the apostles and fathers, along with her apostolic traditions and liturgy, we can confidently affirm that she is the true church which our Lord Jesus Christ established.

Signing off,

In Christ,

Joachim Sanish.

www.ingramcontent.com/pod-product-compliance
Lightning Source LLC
LaVergne TN
LVHW021254160826
845679LV00001B/79

* 9 7 9 8 8 9 2 3 3 7 9 2 2 *